Your Relationship to Motion Has Changed

ALSO BY Amish Trivedi

BOOKS
Sound/Chest (Coven Press 2015)

CHAPBOOKS
What We Remembered Before the Fire (above/ground 2018)
The Destructions (above/ground 2015)
Everyone's But Mine (Paradigm 2014)
Museum of Vandals (Cannibal 2009)

Amish Trivedi

Your Relationship to Motion has Changed

Shearsman Books

First published in the United Kingdom in 2019 by
Shearsman Books
50 Westons Hill Drive
Emersons Green
BRISTOL
BS16 7DF

Shearsman Books Ltd Registered Office
30–31 St. James Place, Mangotsfield, Bristol BS16 9JB
(this address not for correspondence)

www.shearsman.com

ISBN 978-1-84861-633-2

ACKNOWLEDGEMENTS
Versions of poems appear or are forthcoming in
the following places:

Esque (Issue 3): 'Cincinnatus'; *Golden Handcuffs Review* (Issue
19): 'Hematoma'; *Kenyon Review Online* (Winter 2015): 'America',
'Ownership', 'Evolution', 'Number Nine', 'Travel', 'Dying'; *The
Laurel Review* (Spring 2015): 'A Thousand Years of Staring' (1-6);
Ocean State Review (Volume 4): 'Mary Todd Lincoln in the
Boudoir', 'William Seward in the Post Office'; *Omni-Verse*: 'Your
Relationship to Motion Has Changed'; *Verse Magazine* (online):
'Manifest', 'After the Derailment', 'Private Revolution', 'Out
of Wedlock', 'Abyssal Studies', 'Agency and Body Acquisition
Syndrome' (as a single poem titled 'Body Map Symposium')

Thanks to the editors of these journals: Amy King and Ana
Božičević, Lou Rowan, David Lynn, John Gallaher, Rusty
Morrison, Peter Covino, and Brian Henry.

Jamie Karolich created a broadside of 'Mary Todd Lincoln in the
Boudoir' as part of a project spearheaded by Margot Ecke and
Ezekiel Black. Thanks to all three of them.

CONTENTS

I. Ann Rutledge in the Dark

II Body Map Symposium

For Mark

I don't know, but I felt a brewing of diverse particles into the whole.

—*Joseph Ceravolo, Preface to* Transmigration Solo.

I

Ann Rutledge in the Dark

Mary Todd Lincoln in the Boudoir

Pursing another kind of want,
we become night

surrounded with noise branded
by opening. You don't sell the steak,

you sell death in doses
measured by ounce. We verify

distance by telling similar stories
about water: how it became air

upon meeting our eyes and how
it covered every inch of

your hair in terror. But what goes anywhere
other than love being buried

below floorboards to a house
in midst of everywhere

and starving, jaundiced? We imagine
skin as a fence, a spark

lighting entire streets with veins
pumping cold sludge along. Our burdens

become mine entirely
or the trouble with lust

is that it's hollow, bursting cells
into a centrifuge to separate it

from genuine soldered contact.

America

One more nightmare and I'm out. I seem to remember you dancing while holding your arm bent back and tensing. Another dream of child rearing and another about falling down into the gravel and being picked up, only to be dropped again. I've said this before and I've said it before.

A Thousand Years of Staring, I.

In the distance, there is nothing in particular,
depending on which direction you face. In my
next example, I'll be using metaphor to show
how I'd rather lock myself in a room than be
surrounded by other people: a stationary wheel
won't rust if you don't spin it. As if first eyes
touching could be repeated, if you're going to
be there, I'm not. Dear you, I lust you, but I'm
better when loathed. Feet make up only small
percentages of bodies but carry so much
pressure that mine have dissolved from a
desire to move, but with no target in mind,
they ache for compression.

Contusion

One more coagulation
of the fingers and the road
shatters beneath our feet. My
hair pulled by noises from
under the hood and the purple
patches of leg I know are
coming. When we speak of motion
in the future, we'll begin by calling
our migrations unskilled because we
weren't heading anywhere in
particular. This can be our
end time.

Breathing

The grass I know is melting and plastic and another
thing: I stopped believing in parchment that was
dwindling and brittle. I popped my lungs out and back
in. This breathing is tense and I don't remember why
we were crying in the first place. And I'll say it before
this next sharp intake.

Listen for the Footsteps

I want to pull my legs up to my heart and burn
them all at once. We could require immediate
infiltration if our arms were to end up behind us in
a fire or a mélange of different noises. If lies go

too deep, we can consume them and make them a
part of our lineage. I have a lingering desire to be
placed on a somewhere-bound bullet but to force it
back into stasis is a trouble worth

waking up to. I cannot complete my own words
without seeing which you want to use first, a
decision taken too hard to remain uncaring about.

William Seward in the Post Office

What begins
in silent gesture becomes aching

and necessary to contain and hide. If
we are kept in halls and doorways,

another kind of line is scattered
and bled for toxins. To direct us anywhere

is to suggest there's a direction
to go in, but nothing works that way,

certainly. Outsides are always ugly,
but we have set frequencies

for making you swoon, just nowhere
to take you and no desire

to be anywhere. Raw mark
for a word suggests

we can be manipulated
by it and any desire behind it:

it all depends on how near
you sleep to me.

Decelerate

Motion is identified
by changing lines and in
the urgency of static. I will know
all turns after the first visit,
my mind engraving the directions
so no change in the weather
can create dissonance or the
desire to put white spaces in the brow
or chest. The inquiry made of buried
remainders leftover from soaking
a plastic lung can be used as a resort
to final derivation. Unlike the hands
slaughtering the muscles of the back,
revolutions require electrical tape or
a finite number of senses.

A Thousand Years of Staring, II.

Tell me a lie so I can rub it into my skin:
moving slowly is the only way to avoid picking
up direction. Your scopophobia gets better as
minutes wear on. I'm afraid to admit I haven't
looked you near long enough to see a real face.
People appear one way to me immediately, but
then I see them: a look in the eyes to indicate
a passing feel, a curl in the lip that shows disgust
or mutation. Don't fear your shamefacedness
as a peak in terror arises.

In the Night

My lungs are bilateral
by design. If you were
going to cross your fingers,
it's too late now: the sun

has come up and shown us
everything we were trying
to avoid. Being near is useless:
an unknown location gives us
the confidence we need to

bury desire in yards. I know
damn well that there's no
spring here.

Ownership

Sometimes, the revolution starts in the yard, but ends in the main house. What wasn't tied down floated back out into the middle of the sea and is a possession gained. If we're counting again, please consider my placement of your fingers the first derangement. The other parts of ammunition are made of words and we know how to fire them at each other.

I'll Be So Glad When the Sun Goes Down

We can pile sensations together
until we lose everything
we knew about them
to our ability to gasp. Everyone
is pulling their lives together

and I want to send a hand grenade
into mine and turn each room
into its constituent parts. I keep hearing

that language is degrading, but
I say it's growing into a new shell,
which is entirely necessary.

A Thousand Years of Staring, III.

Admit you're more willing to look down than meet
my eye. We'll say this amounts to a fear of crossing
roads, of being or going anywhere. I assume being
washed is being stabbed, but with no sensation that
gives us an antecedent. These are not sexual questions,
but a desire to know how twists of wind become
disaster spaces. In making up my mind, I ignored
all advice to stay and reimagine myself as a direct
descendant of people who lined mass graves. I don't
have a hard time getting to sleep, but a hard time
waking up. Going unnoticed is no punishment: to go
seen and ignored is real hell, though. To go is a verb
that implies motion, but directionality is ignored.

Abraham Lincoln in the Yard

Your typhoid, my
bare, hairy legs

sticking out
beneath my short pants

(we had no concept of height
then), and our words shaking walls

before settling in a corner that's lost
to quiet. We are whetted through separation,

though not union, sifting through evidence
belonging to our destruction, but ashes

remain still with no wind to spread them
and no ground to swallow them. People laugh

at my trousers and I free them
via decree, but in freedom they can head only out

with no direction safe. It's no sin to be glad
you're alive, but it is sinful

to live at all if sensations you feel
are submerged. Another story at

another time
revolves around hands grounded

by wires and electric leads
taped to skin. To walk outside

and not know why you're there
with no idea of spatial relations

is normal and is part curing diseases
un-American, part wish fulfillment.

When the Whip Comes Down

In our isolates,
we imagine no one
can bring light into
space, but unfortunately,
we cannot set ourselves apart

and must find a way
into belonging. My way has
always been to pull air from
your eyes and make it
mine, but I know I can't
hold onto this feeling forever: your

relationship to your
paralysis has been renewed.

Evolution

Once language goes beyond understanding what we see, we can create new things based on words we want to use. Our brains grew stronger because we figured out how to boil water and language came from complex carbohydrates. If there were a limit to things going wrong, we'd have to learn new math. If we were to believe all words we hear, we're likely to forget what we knew before our language came to take us over.

I'll Meet You on That Other Shore

Leaving the house
when I'm not meeting anyone
allows me to be a wanderer
and not a tourist. These streets,
which were once covered in feet,
are now silent and aching
to hear more. Everyone is always
headed somewhere,

but I go out of my way to make sure
I don't appear. To follow
is to have no sense of your own,
just a desire not to be lost, but

when one gives up desire
then one can see all distances
together.

A Thousand Years of Staring, IV.

As we walked through hallways, our figures
were pressed into service as figments in a novel.
My greatest pleasure comes from failure and
my euphoria levels are topped off daily. You
were waiting in a lobby and tapping on glass to
signal me. If someone has their brights on, look
to the white stripe at the edge of any road for
a sense of boundaries and closure. This is my
emotional conclusion: I cannot be happy when
I am supposed to be, only when everything
around me is becoming dead cells. Nothing
matters in this measure, only notes which lead
us to the next space, even if there's no ending
in sight.

Hematoma

We need to see the maps
again. There is no central
emotion that remains when
directionality stagnates. Unclenching
the fist is a sign that the heart
pumps too much blood
at first tick. To pretend the moon
gives us only one face
is to place the dull edge of a knife
on a nail's edge
and imagine feeling sifted
through layers.

Gettysburg in Film

All objects
in body are foreign and those that are seen

are reported too late
for anyone to notice. As muscles desire notion,

your relationship to praxis
rests at desire, my desalinated

pucker fish. Words that settle into grooves
in my tongue are usually first out

in case of fire but I send them
into a space built on structures

and not collapses. We remove twang
from notes but leave in all traces of

someone having passed through
without meaning to cause a sense like loss,

which is defined as a resonance of lungs
and kidneys without having to remain

stationary. The static pressing our nails out
carries makers for arching and appearing

in visions brought on by
a release of chemicals

which normally require users
to be sedated by lust.

Marburg

To touch is to create fusion
in a shard of glass. If feeling amazed
is a heavenly attribute, my mouth
agape must be messianic

or wired in series. The feeling
that a growth can become a
significant line parallel this one
leads to a rationing of language
and the emotive nature of silence.

Bring a twisted hymn
to the atlas room. I've seen
the basement room and dropped
a hot spoon.

Abyssal Studies

All their little faces
ask you why
you're back when you
stop risking your life
to words. You can give it
more than that, but no one
recommends exceeding
any maximum overdose. Into my veins,

I can feel each spark, deeper
than any word
has ever gone. My pulse

grows in every direction, with
no sense of where to go,
but knowing it must
arrive. Upon being
collected, blood dries up
and is ready to be fired into
our air and
dispersed.

Ann Rutledge in the Dark

You're taking me
somewhere I've never been though I've been

dying to go: I can't stay as much as
I want. The foldout couch

could support us but my hands
cannot. To find you here,

in storms brewing
and puddles collected

was not luck, but events in series
building to no space

in particular. What I've wanted to say,
I'll say here: let every tusk rip

through my teeth and become
your ears infiltrated by words

I've never used. But elsewhere
I'm thinking I must be on my way

out during daylight
because suns point

no matter where you want
to be and

that's not here.

Cincinnatus

This is my
urban decay: one

hand giving power
away, and the

other getting
back home and

getting on the
couch. In between

fighting and quietly
considering jumping off

the roof with a
bullet in my brain, I

consider a revolution
that will come

no matter how I
handle everything

else. My rebellion
will be private before

it is well-known in
books and movies. Our

version of harm
is another way to

detach our guide
wires before

being caught in the
net, gasps swirling

around us. If I
wanted to stay in

mid-air, I would
have, but I prefer

the net because it
looks good on my

résumé. I don't
believe in promises

or change because
I know my relationship

to desperation
is growing like

cancer in our lust. I
want to find a

wire and pull it
through my hands and

hang from your ears
like my words

already do. Our
best moments were

hardly seconds across
an open room or

sleeping next you
debating whether I

should kiss you
or not. Sonic space

is a new relative
of mine and I

keep it well hid. I
want to get back

to my land and
burn it so

nothing can grow. If
another crisis

comes about, don't
tell me because I

don't want to fix
it: it's your

crisis now and I
won't share it. The

bundle of sticks
in my hands

must be some sign that
I'm eager to fight but

I plan on ignoring
your calls and your

burning home. Welcome
to my self-

destruction: I want
to heat my eyes

until they burst
all over your self-

pity. I'm a
dictator whose relationship

to revolution has
become calcified. Thanks

for sending your most
spiteful sons-a-bitches:

you might as well
have sent Cromwell

over himself (his
corpse is American-

izing). You left the
door open and now

everyone sees entries
only as they want. I

need a mirror box for
the missing half of my

brain causing phantom
pain. If I were going to

slit my wrists, I'd use
your words. All places

look similar to me: the
sensation of losing

an arm. Becoming silent
requires tension

to already exist and
we only know it

in our chests, beating
endlessly, it seems. As

always, I'm waiting
for soft hands to

flay my skin, I just
don't know where

they'd be coming
from or if they'd

take me anywhere
other than where

I want to be. There
is too much

to say to get it
in under any time

limits, so I'll leave
my words for you in

a silver chandelier. Please
come back and show

us how it's
done, old

man. I'd leave my
plow only for

glory, but you're
better than

me. We're
looking back

with our hands
out, grasping away

from any abyss
we're aware of. I

want to inform you
that my idea of

consent is rather
strict: I need a

confirmation written in
blood, preferably not

yours. Bring your
riot to my front

door and I will
smoke you out. This

is a place to be
if you don't want

to be anyone. Your
language negates

my existence, but I
don't mind at all

right now. Our
desire cannot be

vicious enough. Your
body is wired to be

another set of receptors
for pain. All your switches

feel the same to me. Give
me money to workshop

your body. If we could
begin again, we'd

speak in smaller
words that go

somewhere else. The
direction of language

does not meet
directions of speech

and we've ended
up lost again in

pavements of stray
marks across pages

thrown out. At
night, we prefer

to talk heroic, concerned
with message versus

construction. We all could
use a flatter Earth tied

around our waists and
pulling us in close for

a kiss. I'll save you
just this one time. Only

a certain kind of leader
would give up power

without having too. I am
not that kind. I wish

wind blew like this
every minute and my hands

could sit in my pockets
forever, never pulling

them out to tug
your sleeve. Pull my

socks off while
I'm sleeping and

strangle me with them
because I have no use

for a throat
anymore or air

to fill it. My favorite
scene in any movie

involves no words
or people, just cameras

panning fields or
abandoned factories. They

make me feel like
filling my hands

with fire before I
burn off my skin.

What was new
in previous days

has become re-gentrified
by your teeth rotting

away. If love is the
seventh wave, throw me

a cement block. My
relationship to Damocles

has become too heavy
to bear. We must adjust

our voice for a new way
of wearing down the

sides of our ears. I'm
too lost to tell you,

know anything
at all.

II.

Body Map Symposium

Manifest

If we have a plan, it's
unbecoming: we could
do nothing and
let things happen
to us, but that just

isn't how we roll.
Places we fly over have
cities and culture
and cracked sidewalks too.

Lines that form
the right side of your face
want to take me away.
Each inch is covered
in creases and I think
the room wants to sleep
with you. My relationship

to my body
has changed and we're
here to discuss exchanging

faces and making
arbitrary lines
and separating families
with borders.

Starkweather

With no sense of place, we
still see city lights
instead of stars. What we imagine
to be some far off world
is just the remnant of class
struggles. If we're not the center of

the universe, clearly
we're making a huge
mistake. All lights are out
tonight but there's no real
trouble in the heartland.

Number Nine

Your relationship to language has melted down
around your ankles and your toes are soaking in
words you've built up. Too much time wasted in
front of news that seems to echo only the worst
things of our time. We were made for revolution,
true, but we have to step back at times. When the
riot comes, they'll find you anywhere you are or
are not, so don't be anywhere at all.

A Thousand Years of Staring, V.

We need only to know where we are at, not where we're going, to feel secure in absolution. I'm not Catholic, but I play one on the cross. The only difference between you and me is the words that we use and in which order we place our sighs and discontent-laden notions. We could bring a sense of sultry admonishment to our work if we only knew how to draw the letters that make it. At times we look out and at times we see, but most often, we hear edges of our space before we can sense it.

Parasomnia

If we could pretend for a
moment that your hands
were wrapped around my neck
instead of my arms, we'd feel
our chests drop and warm relaxed

pressure release. I'll sell you my lungs,
if you'll have them, but I know
you'll pass them down a line. Getting
together implies a place to meet, a suggestion

of direction and location and a violent
decision about hearts and tongues.
In another moment, we see failure
grasp at a way to hold ground below.

Out of Wedlock

They expect us to come running when lights burn
brightly or ends of words turn in meaningless symbols
and repercussions of other faults. We push to know
how, but only when connected

in series does darkness get purged and then an open
fear is held. With teeth marks drawing blood, only
lust can penetrate doubt. I know places that force
your head back and words that make you sing, but
unfortunately, wind has come in and gotten us lost.

Edwin Booth on the Outside of History

It's a mask

that's been going unnoticed
and finally a crack appears

to form over eyes and in
a nostril — only a trained priest

can see between genes. Getting a handle
on emotions is a sign of

becoming an adult, but letting go
of concern is as well. I'm concerned

my emotions are wrong and
misattributed to other voices

and other secrets
running around houses and

into gaps in walls where
bodies of language families

are buried. If we could bring
lineages together, we'd create

beautiful words, even if they are
made up and appear

ugly to others.

Travel

I always required motion to keep sleep away from
me, though now I regret having missed so much of it.
Regret is part of an average life, no doubt, but I seem
to have more than most. I should have never lifted my
fingers to your skin or seen the inside of your mouth
lit up. What we had was a momentary escape to eyes
but should never have been a practiced, played, series.

A Thousand Years of Staring, VI.

I've been in denial about a great many things
and I know that your eyes upon me is just one:
across tables, behind backs we imagine there to be
someone who can complete our form of language.
In the first few seconds, contact is made only by
temperature and sensing heat, we move closer but
when our eyes meet, we move back to our positions
at the start and try to conquer again. Send your
queen and let me cut her and admit to nothing
at all. "Don't dawdle," you'll say, "we're heading
nowhere and we're late!" but all street noises have
ceased and all lights are off and the people who
were rushing before have stopped to look at us.

Abyssal Studies

Give my skin
its own tolerance
and walk back
to your place
and hide. Another pity
is that we're not
supposed to have
overheard street noises
that filtered in, but we
reconfigured our lives
around the windows.

Poem in the Newspaper

As things
fall apart, new formations

are seen and new letters
are used to make

new words
with new meanings of

new concepts. At other points,
we renew what was already known

and place it in a context
unfamiliar and directed

at the body or any series
in motion. Wanting needs

no illustration: what we
depend on in desire is that

all parties will announce intentions,
 but that's never happened

between us. We should sign something
at some point but there are no

level tables or floors hard enough
for us. In this version of our story,

the hero finds his desire
in a needle and a b-side. We weren't

headed anywhere
anyways.

Body Acquisition Syndrome

For those who look to the sky hoping for a better
figment of this imagined prophylaxis, I want to
hand you my non-vital organs in the hopes you'll
find some new destruction for them.

As my anemia leads me, so does my bile. I want to
discover a reverberation to sink into and become
part of its silicate. I refuse to accept that this is the
last memorized passage that will

make its way into our canon, but only rejected
vowel sounds will please our ears, wherever we
might find them.

Winters

If another rotation breaks down,
the motions we know will be separated
from their necks. Another eight seconds
until unusual sequences pull at the
gravity set aside as extravagant. Desire
is the firing of synapses into the center
of the brain at irregular intervals: I'm
un-happy when I'm not in love
with the mechanisms that begin
to grind against the skin.

Abyssal Studies

Wanting to believe each thrust will be the last, we
speak only in words which cannot be seen. I'll leave
you part of my nails in my will, though I plan to
use them to scratch my way out. I will crawl

in to find where you go, but I know I can come
back whenever I want. As your breath is caught in
my mouth, another desire washes back over my
central arteries: to feel unwanted and forgotten

primes my blood for exaltation. My next perform-
ance will be "The Abstract," a novel in seventeen
words, but on nine hundred and fourteen pages.

Brynhilde on the Run

Got the whole thing
down to numbers,

dismemberment not being the
side-effect of any drug

I am aware of. Learning to speak
in small bursts

to keep from repeating sounds
and phrases known. Comely,

large: we'll join our
fortunes together. My heart,

unrequired until a gap
appeared, beats in wild

rapture. Rewriting the same note
over and over again, until language

loses all meaning and becomes
forgettable sounds. Desire builds up

in hallways and veins, burned
and buried. There's just a meanness

in this world.

Agency

I don't want to steal your lips, just lease them for
my revolution, as private as it might be. When I
press my flesh to yours, I hear tiny music escaping
and ceasing to form notes, much less a sonic

argument. These are supplemental words to a love
poem that was written in a bloody bathtub over-
looking language as a device: how could I be the
last to know?

Watermark

This is my open-ended lie
to you: we'll catch fire
runoff with our hands and
when they need immersing,
we'll coat our fingers in ignition
makeup and become rearranged parts

of another story. We'll be killing
time anyways, when no location
opens to us and we have to find
new constructs of our own.

A Thousand Years of Staring, VII.

Even in a somber moment, with my retinas
detaching, I can make out the outline of your hair
on your shoulder or a way to say my name. Rods
and cones are a form answer to why I can no longer
find edges in the room or on our faces. The world
for the blind must be the sensation of a dream and
flying through it but then finding themselves at
the funeral of a friend and reading an ill-prepared
eulogy to mourners gathered because of their need.

After the Derailment

This is my story of the generations and how they
collapsed and came back stronger than ever. My
version carries with it a stigma and an American flag
traced on your body from the

legs to your collarbones. I know tattoos which create
the most pain, and I want you to become them: a graft
of old skin, inked, and replaced; remnants of a letter
never sent; and covered marks

exposed. Where our organs begin is a story to be told
in flightless language, grounded and menstruated.

Blunt Trauma

The spleen is rotors
of space we believe
to be the beginnings
of hurricanes. Only a relationship
between things we falsify
and measurements known
by sensations they create
at nails to suture the thigh
bone to the soil. Though
prepared ears can twist any
word into the sound of silk washing
across teeth, cannibalized and
indigenous language satisfies
the ruptures in the mouth. At the cut,

only the image of air twisting
into the corner of the room
can cure. Winter children
tend to know they look best in colors
which remind them of being beaten
and having their arms crushed
under the engine.

Caril Ann on My Lap

Anything that spins
in front of me

draws my attention: I guess I
was just bored and he was

exciting, the way the jacket gets
flipped, the cigarette dangling

from his mouth. I think he was
the President or something: I see

no method at all, the horror. For the days
and nights that we were running,

I knew the world
could not hold us. Knowledge

of our emotions draws near and
we may not have to take it

on the road at all, save for just
getting out of here anyways. Every

distance is nowhere and spending
time dwelling is the same abyss

over again.

A Thousand Years of Staring, VIII.

We imagine death as God looking back at us from
an abyss we've reached into, but nerves don't stop
firing right at the last signal: they fire as they
degrade into soil or immolation clears us. These
sensations are just the body fighting evolutionary
return. As we begin again, we see adoration and
want it to be every day, but you end up nostalgic
for silence.

Dying

This is the last building I'll see and the last words I'll read, but I'm never as far from them as I imagine. We used to sit away from it all and pretend that silence was what held us, but now the empty space seems more meaningful than your words ever did. Let me step beyond and see a new design of my choosing. As if made up sounds had some bearing, I squeak to say my name now because it has no meaning that I can defend. My words are yours now and I have no tones to borrow from and call my own. All I have left is a glance that no one sees and a sigh which fits in my chest tightly.

Your Relationship to Motion Has Changed

Having nowhere to go
is the best place to be: I

don't care if crosswalk signals
never let me pass or if rivers

continue to flood. After all terrors,
settled moments have left to

head towards nothing. Welcome to
mediocrity: we've had a table

with a broken leg for you
all along. As another immolation

passes, we see renewed faith in
saints who died normal deaths, poets

who had heart attacks
in their 80s

surrounded by their families. Ev-
entually you have to accept

that things you knew
about motion are long since

debunked and re-mystified
in new ways. All anger begins new life

as damage, resting on benches and
in middles of streets. Days of

wishing we hadn't woken up
have returned to us, having let us go

long enough to know
we would come back. What we knew

about friction has
dragged us quietly back. You can

tell me but I feel nothing changes
by will: only trauma

brings crisis to boil. What we can do
is reach back away from the abyss

and pretend it can't grab us
by our ankles and

pull. Peel skin back
and expose cells

for what they are: atoms
spinning and twisting

to cover void-made
static. What has never been

is an idea that fire
can tie people to land. Say

you'll become refreshed and
air has never felt so light,

but don't tell me surroundings
will remain unblemished: as we breathe

on them, their cells will over grow
and consume all atomic

variables. Bring your knees
up to my chest

and press monoxide
into the room: we can see

it escape and be trapped
by walls that hold us

here too. When we pass through,
we'll be able to see how suns

arced behind us
and brought vision

into this space. I need
another reason

to keep my
diaphragm

from ceasing and becoming
diluted or there is no impetus

to expect neurons
will receive desires

of a body for motion. What
you knew of matter

has dissolved and a new reaction
is to be conjured. I brought

a divining rod from my bed
so I could find a window

to flood the room. Nothing
we can see exists

when we close our eyes,
only freedom to imagine

an empty chair or a
strand of hair

choking all intakes. I thought I
knew everything

about fear, but it seems there is
more to be mastered if silence

can be buried up to its neck. Physics
is the study of time

being replaced
with nothingness and

encrypted. We cannot gather
all coefficients, but we can

divide series into light
and metaphor. All words

needing to be spoken
are spoken today. Our fingers

split and grow
exponentially, covering

our hands and mouths
until every gesture

becomes an act, every utterance
an off-stage cue. Whatever

hard route we come up with,
it's because we imagine

being jostled to be worse
than time wasted. I don't

understand how you
justify your movements,

but I know your
relationship to light

has been redefined
to meet expectations

you've created: it must
always be present

in order to be used; it must
always be hot enough

to burn any fingerprints
away. We cannot

remove ourselves
from distance, but provide

a new version of force: we must
begin from a state of rest. Deforming

at higher altitudes is not
uncommon, barely visible

if glass is curved
to a certain angle, but a desire which

can become overwhelming
if not observed correctly. What

moving forward is
can be defined in equations,

but we cannot express
locationality in numbers,

just skin temperatures. As hues
of a cheek change, so does

will and freedom
from shattered cells: we become

spacial reference
when our bodies

finally go. On my mind
is a quiet afternoon

spent seeing designs
of an ideal life, a second

made of debris left
from other moments. I can

hear wind in the trees
turning, my arms falling slack

and cold. When all other failed
gasps appear, we can

take momentum along
to carry our burdens. What I

cannot see is how
tiny fragments of bone

can become cancer or how,
as division takes place, skin cracks

and falls. It won't be said
by the end, but we were

never as happy
as we were on

night one. As reaction times
change, so too does

delivery of endorphins
across my hands,

which are chopped
and frayed. If love is a

bitch, then being
forever alone is a

dry heat. No matter paths
set, we're always finding

ways around to keep it
interesting and so we're

not reliving tremors over
again. Again, to be consistent

with emotion is to say variation
is inhuman. I can put my

head back when I want and
pretend I never knew

language could play this way,
but no one ever believes me. We

cannot ask to be brought
anywhere, but we can hope

to be somewhere. Nothing builds
to any resolution: it is just a desire

to complete words or ideas,
but ultimately, we go

nowhere all the time.

Notes

The definitions of love are from songs by Sting and The Rolling Stones.

Poems here have tweaked lines from Bruce Springsteen, Basia Bulat, Genesis, and whatever else was playing while writing.

Abraham Lincoln may have anonymously published a poem about Ann Rutledge. Poems in this manuscript swipe a few lines from that poem.

Thanks

Thanks to G.C. Waldrep and Joseph Wood, whose early reads were crucial to the formation of this manuscript. Thanks also to Craig Santos Perez, who was the first to read the manuscript as it went out into the world.

Thanks also to Johannes Göransson, Joyelle McSweeney, Peter Richards (& Aki), Darren Angle, Andrew Bourne, Karen Lepri, Keith and Rosmarie Waldrop, Gale Nelson, Lori Baker, Brian Evenson, John Cayley, Michelle Detorie, Jessica Smith, Gillian Devereux, Kate Schapira, Kate Colby, Darcie Dennigan, Gabriel Gudding and B.P. Sutton.

Thanks as well to Jerome & Diane Rothenberg for their unending love and support.

Thanks to Brown University's Program in Literary Arts for their support. The original version of this work was submitted as an M.F.A. thesis.

A special thanks to Forrest Gander, the late C.D. Wright, and Jenn, without whom none of this would be possible.

CPSIA information can be obtained
at www.ICGtesting.com
Printed in the USA
FSHW022354261218

9 781848 616332